Circumference of Light

Also from Dos Gatos Press

Wingbeats: Exercises and Practice in Poetry

Wingbeats II: Exercises and Practice in Poetry

Bearing the Mask: Southwestern Persona Poems

Lifting the Sky: Southwestern Haiku & Haiga

Letting Myself In, Poems by Anne McCrady

Redefining Beauty, Poems by Karla K. Morton

Circumference of Light

Poems

by Bruce Noll

🐈 Dos Gatos Press 🐈
Albuquerque, New Mexico
www.dosgatospress.org

Circumference of Light

Copyright © 2016 by Bruce Noll

ISBN13: 978-0-9973966-1-4

Library of Congress Control Number: 2016950805

All rights reserved. No part of this book may be reproduced in any form without prior permission from the author, except by reviewers who wish to quote brief passages.

First Edition

Cover Painting: *Circumference of Light* by Vasili Katakis

Interior & Cover Design: David Meischen

The author wishes to express appreciation to Tom Keyes — for assistance with the original manuscript.

Dos Gatos Press
6452 Kola Court NW
Albuquerque, NM 87120-4285
www.dosgatospress.org

Dos Gatos Press is a non-profit, tax-exempt corporation organized for literary and educational purposes. Our goals are to make poetry more widely available to the reading public and to support writers of poetry—especially in Texas, New Mexico, and the Southwest.

For Ethan

All he wanted was
to find again that
box of sunshine
which had
disappeared from
the kitchen floor
one rainy day.

He loved to sit
and relish that
privacy of warmth,
held there coddled
by some angel's light.

Contents

The Quiet Footman

Word Swirl	3
Dream of a Dead Son	4
Interference Call	5
Atoning	6
Missing the Nail	7
Missed Lesson	8
The Testament	9
Auto Mechanic Connection	10
Upon Being Told of an Unexpected Death	12
The Cold Secret	13
Doing Duty	14
Not Yet	15
Stevie	16
Cosmic Dark	18
Like a Tarzan	19
Deaf Ears	20
Posted	22
Take My Hand, Lord	24
That Beggar	25
Consuela Talks about Pain	26
On Burial	28

This Man in the Mirror

Week Moments	31
Bedtime	32
After the Party	33
The Privilege	34
Bad Start of a Weekend	36
Do Tell	37
Muck of Days	38
Portraits of Selves	40
Everett	41
Anesthesia Dream	42
One with Stone	43
Journey	44
Intrusion	45
Men's Faculty Locker Room	46
Human Body Exposition	48
Etymology Lesson	49
Soft Sell	50
In Costume	51
Making Impressions	52
Readiness	54
What Was Done Today	55
There Will Come More Disconnect	56
Not Getting It	57
Not Quite the Twenty-Third	58

Small Praises

Book Find	61
Small Praises of Spring	62
Toad Stool	63
Phylogeny of Me	64
Tradition	65
Backyard Pond Cleaning	66
Newborn Damsel	67
To Mary Oliver	68
Junk Drawer	69
Overdue	70
Rio Grande Safari	71
Giving in to Wild	72
Little Red	73
Stone Pines	74
Watchers	75
Nature's Nonchalance	76
Robin Hope	77
Double Play	78
Ear to the Big Bang	79
Party's End	80
Royal Visit	81
Gentle Passing	82

Circumference of Light

Found Art	85
Light Play	86
Surety	87
Circumference of Light	88
The Night Listens	89
Still Looking	90
Need for Clearing	91
Welcome Sign	92
Three Miles East of Mitchell	93
Longing in November	94
the mind dissolves	95
Urge to Move	96
Parting of Water, Parting of Air	97
Row Your Boat Gently	98
Circle Line Tour	100
The Time	101
Finding Way	102
Preparation Thoughts	103
Rising	104
Thought on Walt Whitman	105

The Quiet Footman

Word Swirl

I wait for the feel
of words hiding
behind the tree
or rising in bubbles
from a swamp.

Their meanings
come later,
from patience,
but first
the taste
and sensation

of syllables twirling
in the mouth
before their
sounds are
let out.

Dream of a Dead Son

So you come back now
under the guise of wanting
to sell your old chainsaw
and what's this? — maybe
your beaten down car?

I know that cautious look,
worried that I'll blame
or want some explanation
for why you've been gone
but, being the prodigal's
father I am, I don't question.

The chainsaw is not the
McCulloch brand I used to use,
so you start to explain the
differences, intricacies I
should know and things
to avoid so it will not
kick back into my face.
It seems to be a bigger
animal than I should handle
at my age, so I'm not too sure.
But I'll buy. Being Dad, I'd
like to help out.

Next time you come around
I'd love to have more of a talk.
You know, just anything.
Or maybe hang out over a beer.

Interference Call

on the impropriety of interrupting Nature

The hawk slammed
the young robin
into our sliding glass door.
We rushed to see the stunned
fleck-breasted bird
fluttering into its death,
its hunter scared from the deck.

We watched the robin till it lay still.
I picked it up by its feet and
tossed it over the back wall
to where insect carrion eaters
could complete its cycle back to earth.

The hawk returned,
looking for its meal,
then perched on
the outside patio
eyeing me, the thief,
cowering behind the window.

Atoning

For the sin of self-blame,
said the priest,
flagellate seven times
a day for a week.
Do it in secret the first two,
the next five in the street,
at noon,
but don't be arrested.
Go in peace.
You're sure to feel
God's blessing soon.

Missing the Nail

A carpenter told me that
it wasn't the hammer
missing the nail but
the last-second movement
of the fingers that caused
a ricochet onto my thumb.
His assessment did little to
lessen the pain. In fact, it
increased the shame when
I did the same the next day.
Let me just say
you don't want to
hit a blood-blistered finger or
thumb or anything with a sixteen
pound Craftsman's ripper
or a Stanley curved claw.

My thumb lost complete
confidence in me.
Like a dog that'd been
whupped more than it should,
the thumb cowered under my palm
wherever I went, whatever I did.
It was afraid to come out for
months for fear of being bumped
and had to be coached out
even to hold my sandwich at lunch.

Missed Lesson

I'll never show my son
how to die. He beat me to it.
Or should I say,
the bullets from others
got there first.

I tried to show him
in feeble ways how to live.
Maybe I did.
He'd found a separate path,
well hidden.

So what's been learned,
what's been forgiven?

The Testament

Once my aunt showed me a letter
from a soldier who had seen her
first husband die in the war in Italy.
Tony took one in the head.
It was quick was what he said.

I know now that she wanted
me to know more, had waited
for me to ask what that
young soldier was like.

She needed me to give an excuse
for her to speak about the Tony
I never knew, wanted to relive
the plans for life they'd made,
for a few minutes to hear words
out loud to bring her first love
out from the past.

But I was too self-absorbed
to help her open that door.
I didn't know what to say as she
wiped her eyes.

The paper fell back into its forty
years of folds where it had
been pressed in an old Bible.
Don't tell your Uncle Phil I showed
it to you was what she said.

Auto Mechanic Connection

My son is working on
an '89 Jeep Cherokee
he picked up cheap.
It sits on risers,
the front wheels off,
tools set on a laid-out towel in the dirt.
I don't know where he learned this stuff.
I never got past a hammer, pliers
and a screwdriver.

He's glad to see me, to show
how things are going, and grabs
a metal plate he calls a rotor
in his greasy hand,
the part that needed to be replaced.
I see how thin and chipped
it is in spots and recognize the new
one for comparison he's installed.
*I see you've already got the new
pads on,* I say, glad to show a bit of knowledge.
I crouch down to look at this world
of steel and iron engineering under the
fender, marveling at what he has tackled.
I see something shiny new and say,
And you've replaced this, the . . .
He rescues his old man—
*Oh, the flex hoses . . . yeah,
the old were all dried out.*

He lifts the hood and falls into a strange language
of parts and gadgets, sounds that I have heard
before but never understood.
He starts to name tangles of wires
and tubing and other elements.
Weird words unwrap from his
mouth like some foreign tongue.

He shows me with an element of
satisfaction the air filter he's rigged up in a box,
explaining that the air had been channeled back
to the engine but now he'll direct it
out for more power.

Where did you learn to do all this? I ask.

*It's not hard. Hell, Dad, you come to realize
a man made this, a man can figure it out.*

Upon Being Told
of an Unexpected Death

You never noticed before the intricate
needled-lace in the doily on the table
or the grain in the marble on the
countertop as tears bead the surface.
How silly, you think, wondering if
salt will erode the stone or somehow
dissolve disbelief and grief.

The Cold Secret

Aurora Borealis came to us
one forty-below night in North Dakota.
Snow blocked the unplowed way to home.
My brother and I walked behind
our parents on frozen drifts
the last hundred yards from Brinsmade's
main street to our house.

As we stepped from the last street light,
radiating waves of color engulfed the sky.
My mother, in awe, pointed straight up
to a hole cradling stars at the
crest of the array of ribbons.
*It's as if God is calling us
right to heaven,* she whispered.

I looked deep through the wavering
tapestry above, my head bent back
against the thick collar of my coat,
breathed biting air through a scarf,
expecting to see a glimpse of paradise.

All I took in was the great mystery
that still beckons me each night.

Doing Duty

Once in the middle of
a twenty-below blizzard
I drowned newborn puppies

in a bucket of water
while their frantic mother
stayed in the warm house.

I thought it would be easy,
that they would gently
fall asleep as one by one

I held them under
the surface. Their struggle
was fierce. I felt

the young muscles fighting
in my hand, heard the bubbled
yipping fade to absolute silence.

The wind of storm
ceased its howl and all
the world turned to ice.

Not Yet

He was there again
last night, the quiet footman
waiting by the bed.

In all that quiet
on the edge of dark he knew
I lay still, not dead.

I was full aware
of his indifferent patience;
neither of us spoke.

It was not my time
for him to bend and help me
slip into that yoke.

Stevie

We never sat, none of us,
until Stevie had set himself
at the table. Mom would
never allow otherwise.
At Sunday dinner he'd
unfold his napkin methodically,
taking care to tuck it under his chin,
the way he'd always had it done for him
when he was a boy.

When Stevie was sixteen
he'd help Mom make cookies.
The rest of us would come in
from the field and he'd be grinnin'
proud with one of Mom's old aprons on,
brown sugar and flour on his face,
dropped raisins like little squashed
bugs on the linoleum beneath the table.

Bob, the oldest of us kids and
the one who never moved away,
stayed and farmed the place with Dad.
He'd read in the winter to Stevie,
mostly dog and horse stories,
which neither of them ever tired of.

Stevie got so he had his own
crop of chickens and would take
care of them with such love that
he always got the biggest and best eggs.
We said it was because he was
more faithful than a mother hen.
Some people would even drive out
from town just to get some of Stevie's eggs.
Mom and Bob helped him keep his money,
let him choose stuff, little toys

and gadgets from the store.
One Christmas he surprised us all,
gave us each a special colored pair of sox.
We all cried and laughed with him
around the tree. Never did figure out
how he had pulled that off;
even Bob claimed ignorance.

But holidays become memories
and seasons blur together.
Things fell apart when Mom died.
Stevie tried to bury himself four times.
First time Bob found him out in the
shelterbelt with a posthole digger,
said he only wanted to be with Mom.
Dad and Bob seemed to manage with Stevie
over that next winter, but in March
Dad had his stroke and went to the home,
where he didn't last. Being away from
the farm was just too much for him.

Well, Stevie just got worse and
even more confused after that 'till
we had to send him over to Yankton.
That killed him. He withered and curled up
like a corn leaf just before harvest.

When they brought the casket
home before the funeral and
Bob saw Stevie for the last time,
he cried like a lot of people
thought never possible for Bob.
We were relieved when he decided
to remodel the house, got a different tractor,
traded in the pickup and started
going into town on Saturday nights
and church again on Sundays.

Cosmic Dark

We now know every galaxy
has at least one black hole
sucking the light of stars

like the depression that
all of us carry as we spin
and busy ourselves to keep

our energy flowing outward
before we collapse in upon
that ultimate dark weight.

Like a Tarzan

A lion has been following
me in the forest and runs
ahead sometimes to leap
upon a rock face. He is
young, lithe and limber.
We have no fear of one
another and he seems to
like my companionship.

He watches with yellow eyes.
I do not make sudden moves.

He is my protector
and I look out for him as well.
I hope soon I will be able
to touch him, put my face
into his mass of mane and
run my hand across his back.
The beast arouses wildness
of something I've lost.

Deaf Ears

My oldest son and I walked our
neighbor's field a day after the corn picker
had gone through. We strode frozen stubble
rows to gather dropped or missed ears
to fatten our pig for slaughter.

I was reminded of and told
the story of Ruth, Naomi's widowed
daughter-in-law, who gleaned the fields
for wheat following the reapers
and how she was faithful to care
for her dead husband's aging mother.

> *What does that have to do with
> anything?* asked my fourteen-year-old,
> ripe with cynicism. *We're out here in
> the frickin' cold pickin' up corn for a pig,
> an' you go on with some Bible fable
> about two women. What's the point?*

*It's just that we're doing the ancient,
even if it ain't true about Ruth, it's
still a story based on an old tradition.
It's about being faithful and also about
not wasting what could be useful.*

> *Heck, I think this is a waste, a waste of time!
> Pheasants or rabbits could use this corn.
> The pig sure ain't gonna give a damn and
> won't know the difference at what he don't get.*

*But you and I will know. And we will
taste the difference in a couple of months.*

> *This here ear of corn will make the bacon better?
> I doubt that.* He flung a cob to the overcast sky.

You'll taste the difference in that you'll know what we did was right. And you done right by that pig. I think we got a couple of bushels. Let's go home.

Posted

For a few years after
his wife died Russell
left notes for her around the house,
changing them every few days.

On her bathroom mirror he taped:
I'm thinking of you, Gwennie,
have a great day at work.
Yours always, Russ.
(You look great by the way.)

On the back door:
In case you get home first,
I fed the dogs, Sandy's back
paw seems to be healing OK.

Before steeling himself
to empty her closet
Russell pinned a pink
paper to a dress:
Wear this one Saturday night,
I'd love to see it on you again.

Sometimes he addressed them
from Gwen to himself:
Remember, you're invited to
Joanne and Jim's tonight, don't
snack too much. Your Gwen Gem.

The notes ended the night
he came home late with
a new woman friend and forgot
he'd tacked to the door:
Don't wait up, I may be late.
Your GG.

Russell crumpled it to his hand
before she could read.
Who's it from? she asked.
*Oh, just an old friend
who stopped by,* he lied.

Take My Hand, Lord

Verle always said the Lord took his hand,
would wave his steel claw to anyone
who'd listen how he'd been defiant,
even blasphemous, to others'
attempts to talk to him about God.
By golly, he'd run his farm on Sundays,
any day, so long as acres were dry —
until that day the corn picker
collected his right hand, grinding
his fingers like so many yellowed kernels,
chewing his palm to the wrist,
curtailing his world, transforming his spirit.

Over the years the event came to be
an awesome object lesson to his annual crop
of Sunday school boys who'd listen
with eyes opened wide,
his words falling sadly in their ears.
Whether or not God was vindictive
would be saved for future theological debates.
The grain of truth Verle cultivated
was that one must be attentive,
not just to sowing and harvests,
but to voices still and quiet in the fields.

That Beggar

Grief waits all night
on the doorstep
hungry for more
of your heart.

Consuela Talks about Pain

It's surprising sometimes
where anguish can lodge
itself... often it's in the
thoracolumbar fascia
or even the chest muscles and I have
found it stretched out deep
along the femur or tibia,
settled in the gastrocnemius.

Yes, I feel the pain
but you can't take on too much;
you have to protect yourself.
Don't go there, I say.

Sometimes I can almost see
the stress floating out through
the feet or fingers.
Working the occipital cavity,
where all those nerves and tendons
compact into the brain, where
memories, too much load
for even the gray cells, spill out
into the body... yes, I could trace
some of those down, and have,
but how much stress can I
absorb from another person
without hurting who I am?

You cannot massage away guilt;
regret remains bound in some people,
no matter what you do.
Hurt from children, disillusion from
what parents once said or did
cannot be rubbed away.
Grief can be twisted, entwined

around the stomach or spleen
held in the subcutaneous fascia
not just the heart.
I detect it, though that's not
why I am there.
I cannot take it on.

On Burial

Ethan Alexander Noll
21 August 1980 – 4 April 2015

This is worse than
when we searched for you
in panic at a Miami hotel
when you were two.

This is worse than
when you ran away
and we searched for
you for several days.

This is no worry now
but we're filled with grief
knowing where you
are — hidden but safe.

This Man in the Mirror

Week Moments

I was two days late
to change
the calendar this month.
I needed time to finish
September and now
October will be
twenty-nine days long.
It's a pity since
October is my
favorite chunk of fall
and I hate to lose
forty-eight of its hours.
I could borrow those
days from November
but you hate to start
that pattern. Next thing
you'll be playing
with the New Year
and messing up
birthdays or trying
to explain why it's
not your time to die.

Bedtime

I'm watching my wife groom her
hair. Once again she uses my brush
because it is handy and near.
Her strokes are more elegant
than the way I drag the brush
across my scalp when I force
my thinning top to lay in place.

But here there is style.
I love the way she rolls the
bristles through her long strands
of blonde, her eyes closed,
lost in the massage,
combing aside the cares of her day.
I revel in this ritual,
am blessed to be a witness.

Once again she will leave the task
to me to pull out the loosened hair
snagged in the brush from
our heads, a task for which I
think I will never again complain —
to touch and feel the evidence
of our comingled lives.

After the Party

This morning I am left
with extra chairs on the patio,
corks and half-filled cans of beer
on tables. Under the chaise
is a fallen hors d'oeuvre and a
leftover bottle of laughter.
I recall part of a punch line to a joke
that seemed so funny at the time
but now droops limp as dribbled
paraffin on the dead candles.

There is a wine glass behind
the pot of petunias, lipstick
on the rim, perhaps from the
woman in the sexy dress or
the one who talked too much
about her former lover.

I sit and sip strong coffee and
listen to the birds, watch
two robins dig in the grass for
dried clippings for their nest.
A clump of mourning doves
moves about in the dust in
the corner of the yard,
ever wary of me
as they coo gossip they
heard in the din last night.

The Privilege

Often when I string
my hiking or work boot
laces about their eyelet hooks
I flash on Carol Lindquist,
the "older girl" from childhood.
Smart, beautiful, confident — with
long dark hair and a quietness
that heightened her attractiveness.
She was the one real talent
at the town ice rink,
could skate backwards
with grace while the rest of us
wobbled and crashed about the ice.
One Saturday morning I
was in the warming house
when Carol opened the thick
squeaking door and sat a few feet
from me on the bench.
She took off her gloves, parked her boots
beneath the bench, slipped on her skates,
then turned and stabbed
the heel of one blade in
the wood by my side.
Tighten, was all she said.
A sweetness in her voice
made it sound like a request;
no please was needed.
I wrapped my fingers and palms about
her skate and pressed my thumbs
just below each lace hook,
staying in perfect sync with her
as she looped and crossed
the pattern up the white leather.
In a flash a bow was tied
and the other skate appeared.

Again I held her foot and
marveled at her agility,
stunned into nervous silence at
the honor she was giving me.
With an appreciative *Thanks,*
Carol glanced in my eyes.
I like to think there was a smile, too.
She picked up her gloves,
adjusted her stocking cap
and darted out the door.
There is no way Carol could
remember me or the gift she
gave that day. But here at last is
testament — I once helped
Carol Lindquist lace up her skates.

Bad Start of a Weekend

That first afternoon on the beach,
leaning into one another as in
a bad movie, pushing the one
closer to the sea toward the
waves foaming the damp sand,
he went too far,
as she knew he would,
forcing her boots and new
chinos into the February water.
He laughed, saying sorry.

She went away from
the swell and removed the
heavy shoes, tied a simple knot
with the laces, and hung them
about her neck in silence.
She ignored the cajoling,
and then the teasing.
When he attempted to push her
out of her sulk,
to joke her back to his will,
she snapped.

A two-pound shoe with a hard
gripping sole picks up nice
leverage on a three-foot tether,
makes a nice skid on a forehead,
tears the skin open to bleed.

Now it was hers to offer a tone
of regret. It appeared she
was the one who had gone too far,
but her heart was not in the words.
*This bastard better not try to milk
this,* she thought.

Good, he said to himself,
cupping cold seawater to his head,
now she owes me.

Do Tell

For whom would you
place the apple
on your head?

Who
would do
the same for you?

Muck of Days

I sit in the office
of my financial advisor,
dazed by options
for investments, lost
in the jargon of predictability.
I listen as well as I once did
in Economics 101, a class
I dropped the second week.

I stare at a five-story
parking garage across the street
and wonder how I got here.
Not in this office — I mean in this
place in time where millions of
tons of concrete and rebar
support millions of tons of
cars and trucks for people who
work in offices at desks that hold
pictures of spouses and kids.

Everyone must be questioning, right?
In idle moments, trapped in traffic,
watching a cloud formation or
lying awake in the night, wondering.

He advises I move money
from CDs to some other plan
and tells me they'd be safer and better
for interest gain, implying
*For god's sake, how foolish
can one person be?*
Is this what Aborigines did for
thousands of years in Australia?
How does this compare to decisions
Inuits faced twenty-five generations ago?

I shrug and take his advice
and remember where I parked
my car, trusting the man, trusting
the system, trusting I will
find my way home.

Portraits of Selves

This man in the mirror,
I wonder where he goes
when I leave the room.
He appears to be a friend,
but I'd like to know what
he thinks as he flits away.
He could be a hypocrite
like so many people can be —
you know, nice to your face
then laugh to themselves
or gossip to others in secret.

These words on the page
do not always reflect me;
they just rest on a surface,
a façade, and maybe say who
I'd like to be or seem to be
for appearance's sake.
What mysteries we make
behind a glass or screen!
We quick-change our clothes
to be someone else, outright
disappear from view
in the flip of a leaf.

Everett

I held another miracle today,
my tenth grandchild barely
two weeks old. He looked into my eyes
as I hummed a childhood melody.
He squirmed beneath the swaddling.
I pulled his arms free,
let him grasp my finger,
his skin so delicate and tender.
And so we held each other.

Anesthesia Dream

Count down from ten,
the person holding the mask said.
I was eight, going under for
a tonsillectomy.
I saw a large translucent ball
approach, then invert
itself to capture me, and I
drifted off into space,
safe inside the globe.

For years after, I'd go to the
left-hand desk drawer in
my father's study to retrieve
the bottle of red mimeograph
correction fluid that smelled
like ether. I'd unscrew the cap
and breathe in just to have
a sniff of that inner world again.

One with Stone

for J. Gibbons

I am drawn to minerals.
Towers of columnar basalt
call me to an ancient home.

Part of my heritage lies
in conglomerate wedged
between slate and gneiss.

I hear former life in limestone,
in sandstone of forgotten
surf on shores of lost seas.

I am owned by this earth, this
erosion of time we walk upon,
this dust of eras we breathe.

Journey

As sleep transports
to the secret world,
a look or touch

from you brings me
to that place where
I am not alone,

to that kingdom
where dreams are
possible once more,

where hidden paths
become unveiled
to us together.

Intrusion

Down the steep hill
from where I stood in the forest,
a slow movement by a stream.
A young woman, naked,
bathed on the rocks of the bank.
I pierced her privacy
as she lathered and stroked
her arms and breasts,
each in our way enjoying
the sun that fell upon her
through the leaves.
I dared not move — in part for fear of
being seen, in greater part because
I did not want to leave.
She paused in her reverie,
as a deer in the woods will
lift its head to listen and look,
and saw me where I gazed
between the trees.
She stared a moment in return,
then resumed as unpretentious muse,
rinsing clear water across her shapeliness,
not caring if I observed.
It was me who turned away,
exposed, ashamed.

Men's Faculty Locker Room

A retreat from students and women colleagues,
it is here we bare ourselves as the men
we are and boys we used to be after gym class,
after a battle on grid or court.
There's no obscenity or talk about girls or peckers.
We are the academics, the scholars of history
and science; we are the members of the forums
hearkening back to the Greeks and Romans
who steamed over theories about
the cosmos while sitting in their baths.
We scorn the man who dares expose our
sanctum by talking to a lover on a cell phone.
Ours is an Ivory Tower calling.
We vent about administrators
and nonexistent salary raises,
curriculum decisions and deans.
This is our lyceum of important
ideas — where to go for lunch,
how much coaches of our losing teams are making,
how much coaches of our winning teams are making,
or how in the hell did that old professor
ever make tenure?
Such is the life of intellectual gods
who fight off middle-age flab
to preserve whatever machismo
still runs within our veins.

We avoid looking at bottoms
and don't even talk about bottom lines.
No one snaps a towel,
no one wipes another's back.
No one worries if he drops his soap,
but no one sings or recites poetry either
in the lather and spray of the water.

Our thoughts are on loftier matters —
getting ready for classes,
avoiding faculty meetings, and
not losing our grip on our
underwear to puddles on the floor.

Human Body Exposition

It makes a lasting impression.
One could write a poem
"I Sing the Body Elastic"
were our skin and tendons
sealed in plastic

slabs, horizontal,
separated by a butcher's saw
and laid out on a counter display
like a gaping maw

> *I'll take a kilo of that upper thigh,*
> *thank you, and, oh, a bit of*
> *lips and tongue to mix in*
> *when I make alphabet soup . . .*
> *that should make a statement*
> *don't you think?*

Were you or I to be
spread out upon a table,
dead not etherized,
exposed and raw,
the hollow spaces
where our thoughts had gone,
and left for speculation
as to who we loved or
where we had gone wrong,

it might be fun to hear
the suppositions by an
archeologist or plumber
or anyone visiting our array
of nerves and bones.
Don't you wonder
what they'd whisper?

Etymology Lesson

Atone
once meant
to be at one,
as one, as it were,
in harmony
after reparation.

But words
twist like a snake
in the wrong hand
and now atone
might stand to

mean
get even,
twirling back
with a vengeful
bite.

Soft Sell

There's this guy who's been
turning up on my doorstep
each morning selling bullshit.
I listen, unsure if
I'm buying his whole story.

Some days I give him
a couple of pieces of toast
to go with the coffee
or I'll fry an egg or two.
He likes his coffee white,
one cube; I serve it in the same
cup each time, the black one
with the words Phoenix Library
glazed in bronze.

He repeats his stories —
how it looks like he has
a job lined up or he
won't be around much longer
because he heard from
a daughter in New Hampshire
or how he's writing songs again.

Like I said, I listen.
There is a lot of me in him.
I tell him about the projects
I need to do but never will
get to around the house.
We're procrastinators.
He's into scam
as much as I am.
Someday both,
or maybe one of us,
will get it together
and start a revolution.

In Costume

Somewhere, lost among
the long since scattered family
pictures, those black-and-white
Kodak three-by-threes with the
rippled edges that fit into
black-papered albums, was
a snap of me, eight years old,
in blackface, wearing an old
housedress of my mother's.
Dad had burned cork and
smudged it on my face, hands
and arms; lipstick was smeared
to give wide exaggerated red lips,
a kerchief tied about my head,
and off I went to school with
a floor mop saying,
Whall shut mah mouth.

That night my brother and I
tricked or treated
one end of the North Dakota
little prairie town to the other,
coming home with pillowcases
half filled with homemade popcorn
balls, apples, and hoards of candy.
Everyone said,
How Cute! How Clever! —
never thinking twice about the
preacher's boy mimicking the
woman grinning from
the corner of the pancake box.

It was Halloween 1950.
Al Jolson had died seven days before.

Making Impressions

Others at the party fell away
as the woman and I stumbled into the
topic of Monet and she began to make
connections with American
impressionists. I had no idea what
I was talking about but her eyes sparkled
when I mentioned Desch, which was
a lucky guess since a friend in college
shared that name and I remembered
the poster she had on her wall with
the woman in a white dress and bonnet.

It seemed to turn this woman on
that I knew about this artist too.
Yes, we agreed, it was the softness and
use of color that made the relationship
to Monet so.
I took in the tenderness of her skin,
the fine tone of her arms as she gestured
from her sleeveless blouse.

Oh, I ventured,
*and who was it who painted
the children by the water . . . ?*

Hell, there must have been someone,
I thought . . .

    with the ducks?

No . . . this was by the sea . . .

    *You're right! Potthast, he did both.
    In the Park and Children Playing at the Seashore!*

I took a risk:
In a series, if I remember right.
She smiled as if I were a long lost soul mate.

    Not many people would know that, she gushed.

I liked her teeth and the way her auburn hair
curled about her ears and face.
Her voice would be tolerable on long walks,
maybe even over breakfast.

Readiness

Keep a secret arrow
in your quiver:

the point may be
a quick escape.

What Was Done Today

I was with a dying friend
for a couple of hours.
I read him a Stafford poem
about river ice
and then recited
"Sifting in the Afternoon"
by Malachi Black.

We talked and enjoyed
lulls of silence together.
I rubbed his aching feet.

I left and on the drive
stopped for coffee to
think about him alone.

I went home to re-stain
my outdoor deck, again,
in the color called Bordeaux,
wanting to extend the
life of aging wood.

There Will Come More Disconnect

The thought of losing a limb
is not as terrifying as
it might once have been.
When my brother Ken
had gangrene set in his
remaining foot he said, *Hell,
take off the whole limb
above the knee!*

The mind already wants
a divorce from aches and pain,
the heart from slowing muscles.
I look in the mirror and see
that person I've known so long,
who has thinner hair and skin,
a fading light within
to hold back the dark.

We reach a stage where
we can see departing the
body will be as natural
as losing acquaintances or old friends,
as easy as once being able to jump or run,
as we slip quietly out the back screen door
and no one will even know we were there.

Not Getting It

The spirit plays
like a one-stringed banjo,
like a vision of a dead father
who stands silent in a dark suit
leaving answers to your
questions up to you

like a joke you were
never privy to,
you know, the one
about . . .

maybe it's true
the dead laugh last.

Not Quite the Twenty-Third

I am not the shepherd.
I am shepherdless,
wandering in pastures
green with comfort and wonder.
I lie beside streams and watch
minnows and water beetles
traverse their lives beneath ripples.

There is no valley of death.

Amongst these mountains,
antecedents of life roll over forever.
Or so it seems.
Dreams are here
in the mist — in this laze of days —
with no fear of hunger
for questions deeper than sky.

Small Praises

Book Find

I returned to a used bookstore
a few days after finding a poem
buried deep in dusty pages.

I had read it aloud
in the dim-lit cramped aisle,
this glimmer of light on page 140,
then re-shelved the text.

The words would not leave me —
like a woman who said she had love
or that place in the woods secreted
beneath towers of trees that
welcomes you to solace.

The book was still there,
even signed by the poet.
I paid the owner.

The page seemed to open itself,
as if it knew what I treasured.
Over and again I traced its stanzas
of wonder, each time a new marvel
released in images and sound,
drifting up from the print,
a suspended vision of breeze
I could feel in the air.

Small Praises of Spring

No shame in saying
my heart leaped at
the first sighting
of a carpenter bee,

nor at the delight
in greeting the
May grasshopper
on gravel
outside my door.

Toad Stool

Some potential dissertation
datum was deposited
on my sidewalk last night.
I discovered it when I went
to get the morning paper —
a gray dried tube of chitin.
For me it presented
too much temptation;
I had to scope it out.

Let me just say this:
Bufo americanus has an
amazing digestive enzyme soup
to produce such a hodgepodge of
dark, thumb-sized poop.
There were cricket legs
and *Isopoda*, moth wings
wrapped like sushi seaweed
around *Caribidae* elytra.
The shells of centipedes
entangled about what appeared
to be *Tenebrio* remains. Dried
earthworms like noodles.

My petri dish had remains of
stuff I couldn't fit in any order,
but I delighted in cell patterns
in a wing of what had to be a *Calliphora*.
Reading the morning news —
a capsular column of arthropod obits —
so insolently dropped at my door
by one warty plump reporter.

Phylogeny of Me

Phylogeny,
an evolutionary tree
to trace history of bushes,
bugs, panthers, wings and beaks of birds,
to find strands of insights as to why
caterpillars crawl on certain leaves,
to guess at flowers' links to weeds,
see mysteries in fish teeth or horse bones,
query over ambered critters
or shadows in rock — those former
life wonders which slipped into
mud by shores of Permian seas.

I, too, have reversals,
course back across myself,
drop traits of character,
pick up new habits,
alter old patterns, branch out,
sprout stems that lead nowhere,
have extinct loves,
contribute a generation,
join in-groups or out-groups,
switch about in contradictions,
cope with sisters I don't understand,
have my own lineage questioned,
leave littered clues after myself,
fret little about thoughts morphological,
but still try new courses,
flow into those with least resistance,
look for what's comfortable,
what works, what's curious,
what's worth the time,
worth the fight,
until there is that trail,
what's left of me,
an ancestry of myself.

Tradition

I like my toast
scorched a bit on the edge.

My great-grandfather said,
I was told,

*A little charcoal
cleans the gut.*

That's as close as I'll get
to the man I never met:

by digesting his thought
his memory is kept.

Backyard Pond Cleaning

It's a spring chore I don't mind,
wading in the muck to scoop up
the debris of dead leaves
and other plant matter that has
settled beneath the shallow water.
I wear a pair of old running shoes
ragged shorts and shirt and use
the wide mesh net to dredge for treasures
in the stench. The koi and goldfish
scurry and are lost in the stir of dark soup.
I awaken a pair of fat sluggish toads
and plop them on the rock shelf
where they blink in disbelief
in the warmth of sun.
The net fills quickly with sediment.
I let it drain a moment then flip it into
the plastic tub set alongside the pond.
I inspect the sludge and rescue a few snails,
look with care for dragonfly nymphs
and pick out the female *Gambusia*,
the mosquito-larvae-eating fish.
Some of these silver lives are lost
but will add nutrients
to my compost heap and reappear
some summer in carrot fronds.

Newborn Damsel

Sized
to this letter *i*
wriggles the life
of a naiad in the hand
up from the muck
of the pond.

I gently return it
to the water...

and will wait
to celebrate
the beauty
of some later
wings of radiant
blue in summer.

To Mary Oliver

What about the times you
are disconnected, not feeling
so in tune with nature, when
you've lost the sense
of being in the moment
with your work,
with the people about you?
Let me hear of that.

What about offenses by
relatives, by close friends —
how do you place these in
a breeze through birch leaves?
What about the obligatory stacks
that have to be sorted by five because
the boss is sniffing down your collar —
how do you dawdle on forest paths
or sunsets then?

Maybe you don't realize
some of us can't sit by a pond all day
watching whirligig beetles.
Now there's an animal on which
you should contemplate.
Do even you know these
pineapple-scented beetles
see with four compound eyes,
two above and two below the water?
There are a few good metaphors in there
somewhere, but damn, there's the phone again.
I sense there is poetry down under
these papers on the desk but I've been given
the heads-up for an appointment
for which, once more, I'm not prepared.
I wish I could see the world in a multi-view;
I've got the spinning in circles thing down
but can't seem to find time
to sit and ponder too.

Junk Drawer

We all have one,
the place where we put things
with which we don't know
what to do.
The screwdriver we use
to tighten a cabinet hinge
is mixed in with outdated
coupons and that plastic
doohickey that is supposed
to go to something or other
that you don't dare throw away.

Like the brain, there are
memories in there and
emotions you'd rather
not deal with because
company is coming and
you want the place to
look orderly and nice so
you slide it shut: hidden
from view until a guest
is trying to help you look
for a soup ladle or
asks about where you
grew up or some question
you take for prying
about your siblings or
what church you attend.
It's all in there with the
tax notice still sealed in
its envelope and the cache
of broken pencils and
that Christmas photo-letter
from your cousin who
is doing so well in California.

Overdue

I missed it in the corner,
failed to look under
the woolen sweater —

the library book
I took to the beach to read
in June last summer.

Rio Grande Safari

My little grandsons and I took a walk
through the woods along the river.
There were signs of tigers; you could
see some tracks and scratches on cottonwoods.
Alligators could have come up out of
the water at any moment;
there were sliding marks along the banks.
At one place there was an overturned
tree and we looked for treasure
because pirates would have buried
their stolen gold underneath such a place.
Old gnawed stumps were the work
of giant beavers when they ruled the river.
We wove our way past huge anthills
with red and black citizens of the deep
pouring out from their caverns in the ground.
It was a brave and dangerous venture,
and we were lucky to have made it out alive.

Giving in to Wild

Maybe I shouldn't have started talking
about Tarzan's mother to the three women
on the trail. It was when I admitted
I believed Tarzan had been real that one
of them gave a furtive look to another.
They'd heard about strange people in the forest.

I rattled on to explain that back up the trail
I had just walked there was a view of Kala,
Tarzan's ape mother, staring out from
a large boulder that formed the shape of
her majestic head.

Hmmm, murmured one of the trio,
sounding calm and rational, *I've hiked up here
a lot and never saw that . . . Of course, I wasn't looking . . .*

Exactly, I said. *Half of it is in the mind anyway,
but when you are here at the right time of day
and the light hits just so . . .*

They began to look more nervous, so I asked about
the condition of the trail from where they'd come.

Good, they said in unison with quick exchanged glances.
Then, *Are you going up to the peak?* one asked.

*Not today . . . Got a late start.
Enjoy the rest of your hike, and don't forget
to turn around and look for Kala.*

Ah . . . we will, they chimed as we continued
our steps in opposite directions. I waited
till they were out of sight before letting out
Tarzan's victory cry of the great bull ape.

Little Red

The astonishing
thing about that squirrel,
the baby red squirrel I found
that curled in my shirt pocket
and rode with me on my bicycle
and drank from the tiny bottle
and sat in my hand to eat
was,

in those months after its release,
the way it would come down
from high in a tree at my
tsk-tsk-tsk
to get peanuts from me.

Stone Pines

These Portuguese pines
have a way of growing
into you, sending roots back
to the core of past lives.

I like the way their arms
entwine like memories,
twisting thoughts to
where we think we used
to be or who we were.

They breathe the sea from
morning mists, adding vigor
to lengthy limbs that
could bear a thousand swings.

The rings of years are here,
calm, steadfast, outlasting
time you and I will never see.

Watchers

The gorillas looked over
to other visitors and me
across the barrier at the zoo
with such sad eyes today.

They sat, posed in deep
thought, ignoring cameras,
the pointing of jeering fingers
and rude taunting displays.

I sensed they were sorry —
embarrassed for us —
so stilled they did not
know what to say.

Nature's Nonchalance

It is the temperature
of the alligator egg
that determines
the sex of the hatchling.
If the nest in the second and
third incubation week is
eighty-six degrees or cooler,
all females will emerge;
ninety-three or warmer
will alter the embryo
to make all males.

Why nature finds this workable
is still up for speculation.
So far the alligator isn't telling.
She keeps ancient clues
to the riddle deep within her
leathered head
as she lies on the mud in the sun—
and oh, so smug with
her overbite grin.

Robin Hope

By the look of things
the pair of *Turdus migratorius,*
robins as we call them,
had a glorious brood.
I'd watched them gather supplies
of twigs and grass and mud
weeks ago and take them
to the dark foliage in the yard.
And here, this morning,
four juveniles are pawing
the chips of ground cover
with their mother looking on.

They still have spotted breasts
of down but show a sporty
confidence as they hop and flit
around, challenging one another for
grubs or beetles one of them has found.
People who study this species and their
longevity say only one of the four
will make it to November.
While I for one don't want
the world encumbered with robins,
I'm cheering for my local team
this morning, hoping the new quartet
will still be dancing come next spring.

Double Play

The grasshopper spits
tobacco juice as bad as
a baseball hitter

mad at a one-hop
over to shortstop into
an easy two-out.

Ear to the Big Bang

*Found poem adapted from
Ross Anderson's article in* Scientific American,
October 2013

Our planet is a terrible place
to observe a Gravitational Wave.
Its crust is constantly awash
in seismic noise —
booming tectonic collisions
beneath the Earth surface
with sloshing oceans atop.

All this shaking and quaking din
can drown out the thin
matter-shifting wisp of
a million-light-year-old tug
coming across the cosmic sea.

Party's End

After the guests have left us
with the last of the night cheeriness,
soft jazz still on the stereo,
wine glasses in the dishwasher,
the house personality returns
from behind the sofa,
reappears from the
closets where it's
been cowering for hours.
Routines find that it is safe
to come out and settle
at tables watching the last
of bottles and trash
leave the backdoor.
Now begins real conversation
about what has been said:
who brought a good time,
who brought the best wine,
who would not be invited again,
how happy we are to be alone once more.

Royal Visit

No rock or icon,
no little or large deity
gives me clarity
and infinite connection
as well

as that orange and
hairy Tachinid fly
that explored the
cheese and honey sandwich
I held in my hand
yesterday in the forest.

It crawled on my finger
then flew to my shoulder
then back to the tip of my
thumb that became

a momentary throne
to survey this minute
part of its kingdom.
It buzzed away into
shadows of trees
and did not return,
leaving no message
that I could discern,
the same as would some
errant emperor
or parasitic savior
or contemporary god.

Gentle Passing

Granada, Nicaragua

The woman yawned from the horse-drawn carriage
as she passed the coffee shop where we sipped cappuccinos.

I don't know why I think of her several days later
as I sit beside a mountain lake bordered by thick forest.

She was nothing more than one of those passing thoughts
which linger like tiny eddies twirling to nothingness in a stream.

Even now a low mist of clouds brushes across the trees
and causes ripples on the water in the foolishness called time.

Circumference of Light

Found Art

Adorning the window sill,
a scrap of wood found by
my second son on a woodworker's
floor some twenty-five years ago.
He saw in it the silhouette
of a goose and painted
it with watercolors,
gave the bird a mustard body,
splotched in black eyes,
and colored gray and red wings
just so — so that even now
they want to open
and carry me like a dream
to a far-off place.

Light Play

Light only wishes to color
all day and go out of the lines,
to spread hues on floors,
scribble for fun on walls
and draw images of clouds
that sweep across mountains.

It rides with delight,
crosses waves in rivers and seas,
then daydreams upon
ripples that wrinkle a pond
while it shimmers on
grasses and leaves.

Surety

But a distant speck in the cosmos,
though stark, cold, remote,
we are encompassed by light.

Trillions of suns, billions of universes
send an infinite time of glow,
holding us upright and sure.

We walk in trust
steadied by matter
dark, lonely or bright.

Circumference of Light

after the cover painting by Vasili Katakis

An orb of lightning
can zing across a room
and splatter on a wall
to bring a blast of
momentary sunshine
to the indigo
of midnight storm.

But *here* that
single wisdom of pearl
which all along lay waiting
in a delicate place of peace,
where no one paused
or cared or dared
to bend and see ...

Or can this be
that sacred place
where jewel of truth,
becalmed by softened hues,
hovers beneath labial folds
where only hush
and sigh are known?

The drops of life
are everywhere,
in pollen on stamens,
in the corpuscles
of your blood,
in a splash of the sea,
the globe of your eye,
in the cosmos of eternity.

The Night Listens

Forget the thousand eyes.

The senses of smell
and hearing are alive
in the dark when fear
and imagination deepen.

This is another way
of seeing, becoming,
being comfortable
in blindness.

We are all
listened to by something
as much as the listening we do.

Still Looking

I will not be one of those old men
whose eyes sparkle through cataracts
trying to focus on women in the square
who chat intensely beside friends,

nor will I be jealous of youth passing by
in their love on the way to a carefree future.

I'll resist temptation to offer advice
about children or how to change directions,
for directions will change or not, depending
on circumstance more than will.

There will be tragedy and incredible joy
beyond the hill, though the day
breaks gray or whispers promise.

Look for me, the one sitting alone in a park
or along a river. If you should pass and ask,
How's it going? I'll say,
The question is, what has gone?

Need for Clearing

The thickening green wall
creeps its annual invasion
of the meadow until one year
the farmer in disgust says, *Enough*.
He brings out the saws and brush
cutters to re-stake his claim
for hay and clover flowers.
His need for a patch of openness
to wile away his nights and hours
of snow-filled days will not be caged.

Welcome Sign

Space station folks
keep their outside lights
aglow
through every
forty-five-minute night.

They never know
who might
drop in to say hello.

Three Miles East of Mitchell

In the abandoned farmhouse
we fixed up and lived in
for two summers we
would lie in bed listening
to the occasional car passing
late in the night;
the whine of tires
against the old highway
would become louder and higher
in pitch as the vehicle came closer.

The headlights made shadow
silhouettes of the sunflowers from
outside the window move across
our bed and walls increasing in speed
until, in one climactic crescendo,
the room turned black
and the car faded
to a distant swoosh leaving us
in silence to wonder where
our lives were taking us.

Longing in November

I like to see the March
ice floes on the river
when the snow melt
pushes the current
up its banks
and the ice cracks from
the pressure
and the white-blue islands
begin their
southern dissipating slide
to open the eyes of spring.

the mind dissolves

snow to ice,
ice to water
to mist

the myth
of ancient Adam
reminds us

we came from
mud or sea
and will be

welcomed
home to a
hearth of stone

Urge to Move

Waiting for the
flap of the flag,
a wisp of breeze
to take us out
from these waters,

to weigh the anchor
of stagnancy,
to see and smell
rolling whitecaps
and feel that moving
force of wind in masts
deep in the bones,
sailing out to where
the thrill of destination
is alive once more.

Parting of Water, Parting of Air

The liquid is thick enough
to pull my way through —

each index finger feels
the surface, leads the hand

down into softness,
arm sweep, arm sweep,

breathing one with the fluid
pool of eternal blue,

light interacting with molecules,
life interacting with its source —

seconds tick the minutes,
bubbles click the ears,

minutes become scores
of measures and if you think

to look, the clock will have
lapped itself a few more times.

Row Your Boat Gently

Life may not be
just a dream.

However,
on the chance
that it is...

keep on your
merry way
and enjoy
these moments.

Wynken, Blynken
and brother Nod
found bliss this way

and Mahler flowed
through the loss of
his daughter by writing
his sixth masterpiece

rowing through grief
as did many great
artists and poets
unknown and known.

So do row,
row on as if
adrift on a
Monet pond

through glorious
lilies, row on to float
beneath a
Japanese bridge,

row on, gently
upon sweet Afton,
fulfilled,
row on in the dream,
row on,
row on even into
the dream of death.

Circle Line Tour

Coming off the Harlem to
the East River my young son
said, *Dad, look at that!* and
pointed to a bloated corpse
bobbing in our wake,
heading past Manhattan's
wharves on its voyage to sea.
The tour guide on microphone
saw it too and was quick to direct
attention to features in the Bronx
and down the way to Brooklyn.
But my son and I watched
the peaceful floater
dissipate into the rising and falling
rhythms of shadows and sparkling light.

The Time

When do we know
it is time to walk
out on the ice floe

to that great flat
white horizon of
forever silence?

Is it when the seals
have become scarce
or caribou abandon

their annual trek
and you see
the grandchildren are thin?

Is that when you
or I will wander
to be lost in the

polar night of
the radiant colors
of frozen light

and ascend
to the sparkle
of constellations?

Finding Way

> *Where is the night*
> *when the sun is shining?*
> *If it is night, then the sun*
> *withdraws its light.*
>
>   Songs of Kabir   XXXVII

the night presses
deep in the self

the eye of the staff
feels roots and rock
in the path while

other eyes stay alert
to the tap-tap-tapping
of your stick

even stars
cast a shadow
when eyes are wide

Preparation Thoughts

Today I think I would like
to be buried in a forest.

Yesterday I thought it would be okay to
be rocketed beyond the atmosphere to
speed my return to cosmic dust.

A casket in the sea never appealed to me.

I get the feeling most days that it
will not matter, whatever the end may be.

The electricity held within
these chemicals of me
will be dispersed in a flash of light,
and light is one of the universals
and does not disappear.
What we call dark is only light
that has traveled somewhere else —
dark is an empty avenue, an open
pathway for suns and galaxies of souls.

Rising

Not at all
a downward slope,
this aging through years.
We are pushed up
towards the top,
buoyant with memories
where even pain hoists
like a crutch. Much has
been felt, too much seen
sometimes, yet we rise
like cream in a bottle
left by some milkman
on the top step, waiting
for a child to open the door.

Thought on Walt Whitman

He sings on to us
two centuries past death,
resonating our hearts,
still tuning our souls
to who we are
and can become.

Comforting, probing,
leading, confusing,

and challenging
with gentle love,

he puts his arm
about our shoulders
and whispers,
Whoever you are,
Keep on.

About the Author

As a child Bruce Noll wrote rhymes and memorized other poets' verses, discovering music and fluency in the sounds of words. Born in New York, raised in Minnesota and North Dakota, this son of a preacher spent countless hours on the prairies, in woodlands, and alongside the Mississippi River. In his early twenties, Bruce discovered *Leaves of Grass* — the magic of Whitman — which has had a steadying influence throughout his life. In 1970 Bruce created "Pure Grass: An Experience with Whitman's Leaves." For more than four decades — in twenty-seven states and six countries — his performances of "Pure Grass" have carried the transforming words of a great voice to poets and non-poets alike. His website — brucenoll.com — is a repository for "Pure Grass" and Bruce Noll's dedication to all things Whitman.

A family man, Bruce lives in Albuquerque, New Mexico, with his wife Betsy. They have ten grandchildren.

Acknowledgments:

"Phylogeny of Me," *HMS Beagle,* 2000.
"Stevie," *South Dakota Magazine,* 2000.
"Take My Hand, Lord," *South Dakota Magazine,* 2002.
"Bad Start of a Weekend," *Conceptions Southwest,* 2006.
"To Mary Oliver," *American Entomologist,* 2010.
"Circumference of Light," *Now SEE/HEAR,* 2015.

Also by the Author

The Gospel Edits — poems
Notes to My Mortician — poems
American Entomologist *Poet's Guide to the Orders of Insects* (co-editor)

www.ingramcontent.com/pod-product-compliance
Lightning Source LLC
Chambersburg PA
CBHW070630300426
44113CB00010B/1728